SOUTH DAKOTA

MITCHELL CORN PALACE

HELLO U.S.A

by Karen Sirvaitis

Lerner Publications Company

You'll find this picture of a pasqueflower, or wild crocus, at the beginning of each chapter in this book. Pasqueflowers grow throughout the Great Plains. The flowers bloom in early spring and signal the end of South Dakota's long winter.

Cover (left): An American bison on the South Dakota plains. Cover (right): Mount Rushmore. Pages 2–3: Hay bales scattered through a farm field. Page 3: The Corn Palace in Mitchell.

This book is available in two editions:
Library binding by Lerner Publications Company, a division of Lerner Publishing Group
Soft cover by First Avenue Editions, an imprint of Lerner Publishing Group
241 First Avenue North
Minneapolis, MN 55401 U.S.A.

Website address: www.lernerbooks.com

Library of Congress Cataloging-in-Publication Data

Sirvaitis, Karen, 1961–
     South Dakota / by Karen Sirvaitis. (Revised and expanded 2nd edition)
        p.   cm. — (Hello U.S.A.)
     Includes index.
     ISBN: 0–8225–4070–3 (lib. bdg. : alk. paper)
     ISBN: 0–8225–4139–4 (pbk. : alk. paper)
        1. South Dakota—Juvenile literature. [1. South Dakota.]
     I. Title. II. Series.
     F651.3 .S57 2002
     978.3—dc21   2001001741

Manufactured in the United States of America
1 2 3 4 5 6 – JR – 07 06 05 04 03 02

CONTENTS

The caves of Wind Cave National Park, such as the Elk Room, feature limestone ceiling formations unlike those in any other caves in the United States.

THE LAND

West Meets Midwest

outh Dakota, a rectangular state, is part of two different worlds. Considered a midwestern state, South Dakota is actually where the Midwest meets the West. It's where wheat fields give way to cattle ranches and where rolling hills lead to mountains.

The **prairies** and farms of neighboring Minnesota and Iowa advance into eastern South Dakota. The canyons and rangeland of Montana and Wyoming blend with western South Dakota. Endless miles of **plains** cover the central part of the state and stretch north into North Dakota and south into Nebraska.

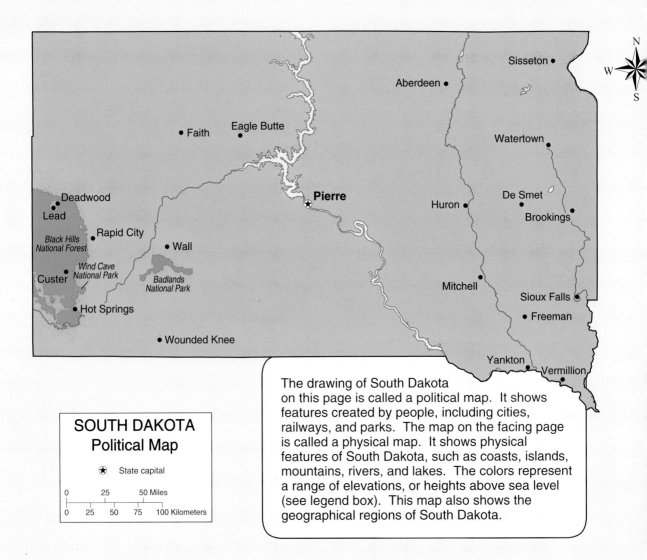

N
W · E
S

Sisseton ●

Aberdeen ●

● Faith   Eagle Butte ●   Watertown ●

Deadwood ●   De Smet ●
Lead ●   Huron ●   Brookings ●
Black Hills   ● Rapid City
National Forest   ● Wall   Mitchell ●   Sioux Falls ●
Wind Cave
National Park   Badlands   ● Freeman
Custer ●   National Park
● Hot Springs   Yankton ●
● Wounded Knee   Vermillion ●

Pierre ★

SOUTH DAKOTA
Political Map

★ State capital

0   25   50 Miles
0   25   50   75   100 Kilometers

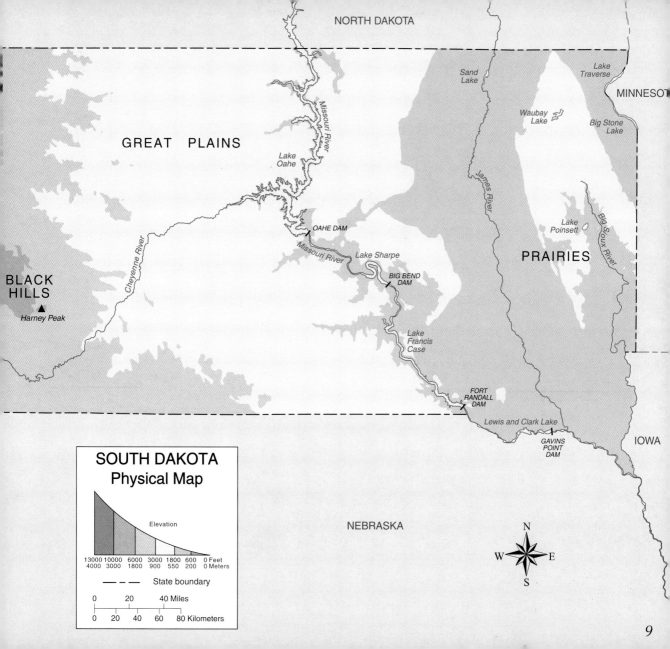

NORTH DAKOTA

Sand
Lake

Lake
Traverse

MINNESOT

Waubay
Lake

Big Stone
Lake

GREAT PLAINS

Missouri River

Lake
Oahe

James River

OAHE DAM

Lake
Poinsett

Big Sioux River

Missouri River

Lake Sharpe

PRAIRIES

BLACK
HILLS

Cheyenne River

BIG BEND
DAM

▲
Harney Peak

Lake
Francis
Case

FORT
RANDALL
DAM

Lewis and Clark Lake

IOWA

GAVINS
POINT
DAM

NEBRASKA

SOUTH DAKOTA
Physical Map

Elevation

| 13000 | 10000 | 6000 | 3000 | 1800 | 600 | 0 Feet |
| 4000 | 3000 | 1800 | 900 | 550 | 200 | 0 Meters |

– – – State boundary

| 0 | 20 | 40 Miles |

| 0 | 20 | 40 | 60 | 80 Kilometers |

N
W   E
S

Sand Lake, in northeastern South Dakota, attracts flocks of birds.

The regions within South Dakota are as different as the states surrounding it. From east to west, these regions are the Prairies, the Great Plains, and the Black Hills.

The Prairie region covers about one-fourth of South Dakota. More than 100 glistening lakes dot the northern part of the region, making it a popular vacation area.

Most of the lakes were formed by **glaciers.** These huge blocks of ice and snow moved across South Dakota thousands of years ago, carving basins into the earth's surface. Gradually, rainwater and the melting ice of the glaciers filled the basins, creating lakes.

Gently rolling hills blanket much of the Prairies. Native grasses, some as high as 12 feet, once coated the hills. Farmers plowed up this **grassland** in the late 1800s to plant crops in the fertile soil. Acres of wheat and corn stretch across the region.

The Great Plains region covers a large area of North America and crosses central and western South Dakota. Hills and valleys extend across South Dakota's plains. As in the Prairie region, the grassy plains have been plowed to make room for crops. In the western part of the state, the land becomes more rugged. **Buttes** (steep, flat-topped hills) tower over the surrounding plains, and canyons weave between the hillsides.

The Great Plains of South Dakota are covered by native grasses.

For thousands of years, wind and rain have worn away the soft, colorful rock of the Badlands, forming deep gullies, high cliffs, and strangely shaped peaks. The Badlands cover about 100 miles of South Dakota's Great Plains.

South Dakota's most rugged landscape is in the Black Hills. From a distance, the region's thickly forested mountains appear to be black. Harney Peak, the state's highest point, reaches 7,242 feet in the Black Hills.

The lowest point in South Dakota is Big Stone Lake, which lies along the Minnesota border in the Prairie region. Big Stone, Traverse, Waubay, and Poinsett are among the state's largest natural lakes. Dams built along the Missouri River have created **reservoirs,** or artificial lakes, including Lakes Oahe, Francis Case, Sharpe, and Lewis and Clark.

The Missouri River is South Dakota's most important waterway. Freighters and barges cruise the river, carrying farm products and other goods to and from the state. Almost every river in South Dakota— including the Cheyenne, the Big Sioux, and the James—drains into the Missouri.

Hikers can view the lush forests of the Black Hills from Harney Peak.

Some waterways in South Dakota may flood during the spring, dry up during the summer, or freeze during the winter—depending on the weather. The state's climate ranges from blistering hot to icy cold. Summer temperatures average 74° F, while average winter temperatures hover around 16° F.

Flowing southward and cutting through the Great Plains, the Missouri River divides South Dakota in half. South Dakotans call the halves of their state East River and West River.

Eastern South Dakota and the Black Hills receive the most **precipitation** (rain, snow, sleet, and hail) in the state. Parts of South Dakota experience **droughts,** or long periods with little or no precipitation. During a drought, the farmland across the Prairies and the Great Plains turns dry and dusty. When the wind blows hard, a dust storm can cloud the air.

South Dakota receives an average of 18 inches of precipitation every year. This amount is enough for native grasses but does not support large plants such as shrubs and trees. Forests cover less than 4 percent of the state. The few trees in South Dakota grow mainly in the wetter Black Hills region and along riverbanks. The most common trees include pine, aspen, oak and cottonwood.

Flowers such as poppies and black-eyed Susans color the plains in springtime. Bluebells, forget-me-nots, and flowering cactuses thrive in western South Dakota.

A South Dakota forest in the spring

A group of pronghorn pause on the prairie.

From prairie dogs to pronghorn, South Dakota is home to a variety of wild animals. Coyotes, as well as thousands of bison, inhabit the Great Plains. Elks and bighorn sheep climb ledges in the Black Hills. Beavers and raccoon live in eastern South Dakota, while bald eagles nest in the Badlands.

Natives and Newcomers

The first people to settle in the area of South Dakota lived at least 10,000 years ago. Bones, tools, and weapons have been unearthed in the Black Hills region and along the Missouri River. These small pieces from the past reveal that the first South Dakotans used spears to hunt large mammals, including sloths and mammoths.

About 1,500 years ago, a group of Native Americans known as mound builders settled east of the Missouri River. These Native Americans are known for the large earthen burial mounds they built along the Big Sioux River and near Big Stone Lake.

Around A.D. 800, the Native Americans in the area stopped building mounds. No one is exactly sure what happened to the mound builders, but many researchers believe they died from widespread disease.

Hundreds of years later, tribes that became known as the **Plains Indians** began to arrive in the northern Great Plains. The Arikara Indians canoed up the Missouri River to South Dakota. They settled on the banks of the Missouri and Cheyenne Rivers. There they built villages, hunted bison, and grew crops of corn, beans, and squash.

After the Arikara came the Cheyenne. Pushed westward by enemy nations, the Cheyenne also built villages, farmed, and hunted along the Missouri and Cheyenne Rivers.

The Arikara and the Cheyenne often met on the banks of the Missouri River to trade furs, pottery, and beads. Every now and then, they also traded

French fur traders sometimes exchanged alcohol for prized furs collected by Native Americans.

with strangely dressed men who spoke a very different language.

These men were French fur traders. They exchanged pots, guns, and tools for beaver pelts, which sold for a high price in Europe. The Frenchmen claimed that France owned the trading grounds, along with much of North America's Great Plains. They called this huge area between the Missouri River and the Rocky Mountains the Louisiana Territory.

In 1743 two French Canadian brothers wrote about the South Dakota region. François and Louis-Joseph La Vérendrye took notes about the Native Americans they met and about the plants and animals they saw while canoeing down the Missouri River.

Not long after the La Vérendrye expedition, the Sioux Indians were pushed westward into Arikara territory by their longtime rivals, the Ojibwa. The Sioux and the Arikara began fighting for control of the Missouri River valley. The Sioux defeated the Arikara and eventually spread throughout South Dakota.

Meanwhile, U.S. president Thomas Jefferson bought the Louisiana Territory from France. The Louisiana Purchase, which took place in 1803, doubled the size of the United States.

Jefferson sent an expedition, led by Meriwether Lewis and William Clark, to explore the new possession. In 1804 Lewis and Clark reached the area of South Dakota, where they camped along the Big Sioux and the Missouri Rivers. The men met Native Americans from various tribes and saw plants and

The Lewis and Clark expedition might never have succeeded without the help of a Shoshone Indian woman named Sacagawea. She guided the American men and helped them communicate with the Native Americans they met, including the tribes living in South Dakota.

animals they had never seen or heard of before. When the explorers returned home in 1806, they reported finding beavers and other fur-bearing animals in the area of South Dakota.

Encouraged by the news, fur traders soon headed for the Great Plains. Although Lewis and Clark had generally gotten along well with tribes they had met, relations between the fur traders and the Native Americans were sometimes difficult. In 1823 the Arikara attacked and killed 13 U.S. fur traders.

To help protect fur traders, the U.S. Army sent troops, who were aided by Sioux Indians, to drive the Arikara northward. These soldiers were the first of many to come.

Originally called Fort Tecumseh, Fort Pierre was founded in 1823 as a trading post. Sioux Indians and fur traders gathered here to exchange furs, hides, blankets, clothing, and household goods.

By 1850 most of the beavers had been killed, ending the fur-trading boom in South Dakota. But another kind of settler was attracted to the area—the farmer.

In the mid-1800s, people from the eastern United States ventured west seeking good farmland. Some of these pioneers built farms on the fertile soils in southeastern South Dakota—the homeland of a branch of Sioux Indians called the Yankton.

To avoid any chance of warfare against the newcomers, the Yankton Sioux ceded the region to the U.S. government in 1858. In exchange, the Sioux received money, supplies, and 400,000 acres of **reservation** land. The government promised that the settlers would not disturb the Sioux on the reservation.

Before long, farmers and businesspeople were pouring into the newly opened area. They built the towns of Yankton, Vermillion, and Bon Homme. In 1861 the U.S. government established the Dakota Territory, which included what later became North and South Dakota and parts of Wyoming and

The Minnesota Uprising put fear into Dakota Territory pioneers. Nearly 600 people died in this conflict between Native Americans and settlers.

Montana. The territory was named after the Dakota (or Sioux) Indians.

The surge of settlers to the Dakota Territory did not last long. In fact, in the following few years about half the pioneers left their stores, towns, and fields behind.

The pioneers were frightened by what became known as the Minnesota Uprising (1862–1866). The Santee Sioux in Minnesota, angry that so many newcomers were farming Sioux land, began raiding white settlements. When the attacks spread into the Dakota Territory, many of the pioneers fled, returning only after U.S. troops ended the conflict.

Red Cloud was a warrior and chief of the Oglala Sioux. He led attacks against forts along the Bozeman Trail in the Dakota Territory. The effort to close the trail is often called Red Cloud's War. It resulted in the creation of the Great Sioux Reservation.

The discovery of gold in Montana stirred up more conflict. Thousands of prospectors crossed the Dakota Territory to get to the goldfields. One explorer, John Bozeman, found a shortcut through Sioux homelands. When the U.S. government built forts to protect travelers along the Bozeman Trail, the Sioux attacked the forts.

The Sioux were successful. In 1868 the U.S. government signed a **treaty,** or agreement, stating that the trail would not be used. In addition, all pioneers west of the Missouri River in the Dakota Territory had to leave. The entire region became the Great Sioux Reservation—property of the Sioux nation.

After the treaty, most of the Native Americans in the Dakota Territory lived on the reservation. Battles and attacks ended, and farmers were again attracted to the rich soils east of the Missouri River.

Some of the farmers were **immigrants** from Denmark, Norway, Sweden, and Germany.

South Dakotan settlers called "sodbusters" used resources from the prairie to build their homes.

Little House from the Prairie

South Dakotans living in areas of treeless grassland lacked a lumber supply. But the roots of the prairie grasses were so solid that these homesteaders, also known as sodbusters, used blocks of sod (or grass) as a building material for their homes.

Called soddies, the houses were cheap to construct. The average soddie consisted of one acre of sod, a couple of windows, and a door. The total cost was about $5 or $10. The homes did not burn down during prairie fires, and they kept out most of the snow, rain, and wind-blown dust. But they were also uncomfortable. Dirt fell from the ceilings, and animals, such as gophers and snakes, burrowed through the floors.

Many sodbusters dreamed of the day they would earn a profit from their crops and could afford to buy lumber shipped from woodlands. But others dwelled in their practical soddies long after wood-frame homes became common on the prairie.

South Dakota farmers have long struggled with grasshoppers and other pests. In the early 1900s, people began spraying their fields with insecticides in order to combat these damage-causing insects.

They had come to the Dakota Territory to benefit from the Homestead Act. Through this act, the U.S. government gave 160 acres of land to each pioneer family willing to plow the prairie. These settlers became known as homesteaders.

In the early 1870s, the farmers of Dakota Territory battled something they could not settle by treaty—grasshopper raids. Millions of grasshoppers invaded the territory's cropland every July for four years. Swarms of these insects destroyed entire crops and drove many farmers out of the territory for good. Some settlers braved the hard years, waiting for better times.

Hoppers by the Hordes

Grasshoppers, the most numerous insect on the prairie, have always been a bother to South Dakotans. The grasshopper raids of the 1870s, however, were caused by a type of hopper that no longer exists in the United States—the migratory locust. For migratory locusts to have become a problem to farmers and ranchers, certain environmental conditions had to be ripe.

A grasshopper's chance of survival, for instance, improves greatly during a drought. A dry autumn extends the egg-laying season, allowing a female hopper to lay more eggs than usual. Disease, which spreads quickly in humid weather, is not a major killer of locusts during a drought. And if birds leave an area that is hit by drought to find food and water elsewhere, locusts have fewer enemies.

During the drought of the 1870s, a swarm of migratory locusts rose near the Rocky Mountains. Aided by the wind, they headed east toward the Great Plains. The warm weather encouraged them to become active. They traveled together and when one swarm met another, dense hordes developed. Some hordes were miles long, miles wide, and miles deep.

When the hoppers stopped to eat, they consumed whatever was in their path, including crops, tree bark, and clothes. Farmers and ranchers did their best to stop the insects with fire, but the numbers—which had reached the billions—were too great.

As the locusts approached the more humid climate in the east, their chances of survival decreased. Predators and disease helped reduce the size of the horde, which eventually died out naturally.

Lieutenant Colonel Custer's expedition made its camp on French Creek in the Black Hills. The city of Custer is located near the former camp.

In 1874 the U.S. Army sent Lieutenant Colonel George Armstrong Custer and 1,200 soldiers, scientists, and miners to the Black Hills to study the area's geography and natural resources. Custer was also required to build a fort to prevent settlers from entering the Great Sioux Reservation.

Word got out that Custer's expedition had found gold, and hundreds of gold seekers poured into the Black Hills. The U.S. government volunteered to pay the Sioux for the right to mine the region. But the Black Hills were sacred to the Native Americans, and they refused the offer. Custer and his troops withdrew, leaving the Native Americans and the miners to fend for themselves.

The city of Deadwood *(above)* became home to more than 20,000 miners *(inset)* and merchants shortly after being founded in 1876.

Sitting Bull, a Sioux medicine man born in South Dakota, refused to ever live on a reservation. He spiritually guided Crazy Horse in the Battle of the Little Bighorn (which took place in Montana)—the most famous battle during the War for the Black Hills.

The miners built several towns near the major gold strikes in the Black Hills. In 1876 these illegal settlements on Sioux land helped spark the War for the Black Hills.

U.S. troops started the fighting by pursuing a group of Sioux who would not live on the reservation. These Sioux were refusing to sacrifice their traditional ways for reservation life.

The major battles of the war took place in the present states of Montana and Wyoming, but the Sioux occasionally attacked miners in the Black Hills. At the war's end, the Sioux were forced to sign a new treaty, giving up the Black Hills region of their reservation.

In the 1880s, the Black Hills drew more miners and also ranchers, who found plenty of grazing land for their cattle and sheep. The ranchers supplied meat to local towns and to the Native Americans. After railroads were built across the Dakota Territory, the ranchers also shipped their livestock to

Sheep and cattle ranchers came to South Dakota to raise livestock for shipment across the United States.

the East Coast to be slaughtered and sold.

By 1889 the Dakota Territory had enough white settlers to become a state. The U.S. government split the territory in two, admitting North Dakota and South Dakota to the Union as separate states.

The beginning of South Dakota's statehood marked the end of the Great Sioux Reservation. In 1889 the United States asked the Sioux to give up most of their land. To avoid war, the Native Americans agreed to settle on smaller reservations.

LET THE
Eagle Scream!
— · —
PIERRE!
— IS THE —
PLACE!

But bloodshed came in 1890 during the Massacre at Wounded Knee, the last major conflict between U.S. troops and Plains Indians. Knowing that their traditional way of life was coming to an end, many Sioux Indians had begun to practice a new religion called the Ghost Dance. Followers of the Ghost Dance believed that health and happiness would come to Native Americans only if people lived in peace. U.S. military officials, suspicious of the large religious gatherings, ordered the Sioux Indians to stop practicing the Ghost Dance.

The Sioux who refused to quit fled to the Badlands, where they were captured by U.S. troops and taken to Wounded Knee Creek. When a gun accidentally went off among the prisoners, the soldiers reacted, filling

Pierre competed with several other towns to be named the capital of the state of South Dakota.

the air with a thunderous blare of cannon fire and gunfire. Hundreds of Native Americans were killed, as were 30 U.S. soldiers.

South Dakota's first years of statehood also were troubled by a period of drought known as the Great Dakota Bust. Unable to make a living from farming the parched land, many settlers left the state. Newcomers arrived after the drought ended in 1897 and as more Native American lands were opened to settlement. To encourage even more pioneers to come to South Dakota, the U.S. government greatly increased the number of acres a homesteader could claim.

Sioux Indians began practicing the Ghost Dance in 1890. This religion, introduced by Sitting Bull, brought groups of Sioux together to express themselves and their beliefs through physical movement.

South Dakota's farmers made a good profit supplying meat, vegetables, and grains to troops fighting overseas during World War I (1914–1918). Crops sold for high prices during the war, so farmers plowed up more of their land to plant wheat and corn.

During the 1930s, farmers in South Dakota again saw hard times. Almost 10 straight years of drought and dust storms, along with several grasshopper raids, ravaged crops. On top of that, South Dakotans were suffering through the Great Depression, a major slump in the nation's economy. During the depression, banks failed, businesses closed, and many workers lost their jobs.

During the prosperous farming decade of the 1910s, many farmers bought new equipment.

Mount Rushmore: An Unfinished Masterpiece

In 1927 sculptor Gutzon Borglum began carving Mount Rushmore National Memorial near Rapid City, in the Black Hills. His project, however, was never finished. The 60-foot monument, featuring the faces of four U.S. presidents, was supposed to include their waists.

Borglum also planned to house a history museum in the tunnel that is located within the memorial. Borglum died in 1941, before he had a chance to complete his masterpiece. Although his son tried to carry on his father's work, the project came to a halt when the U.S. government ran out of funds for the memorial during World War II.

The Great Depression ended during World War II (1939–1945), when South Dakota's farmers were again called on to supply food to troops overseas. The U.S. government also built Ellsworth Air Force Base and Sioux Falls Air Force Training Base, which created jobs for South Dakotans.

After the war, the U.S. government hired workers to build four dams on the Missouri River in South Dakota. Called the Pick-Sloan Missouri Basin Program, the dams controlled flooding, supplied water to cities and farms, and powered engines that produced electricity. The four reservoirs created by the dams became known as the Great Lakes of South Dakota.

In 1973 a group of Native Americans took over the village of Wounded Knee on the Pine Ridge Indian Reservation for 71 days. They were protesting the leadership of Richard Wilson, president of the Oglala Sioux, and hoped to gain fairer treatment for Native Americans across the country. U.S. forces were sent to control the protest. Two Native Americans were killed, dozens of people were injured, and hundreds were arrested before the group surrendered to U.S. forces.

The fight for land, leadership, and freedom in South Dakota has moved from the battlefield to the courthouse. In 1980 the U.S. Supreme Court ordered the U.S. government to pay the Sioux more than $120 million for land seized in the Black Hills region in 1876. The Native Americans have refused the money. Instead, they want 1 million acres of the Black Hills returned to them.

The Spirit of Crazy Horse

Only 17 miles south of Mount Rushmore, the budding image of Sioux leader Crazy Horse astride his horse marks Thunderhead Mountain in the Black Hills. At the request of Sioux chief Henry Standing Bear, the Crazy Horse Memorial was started in 1948 by sculptor Korczak Ziolkowski, who dedicated much of his life to the project.

Once it is completed, the memorial will be the largest sculpture in the world, reaching 563 feet in height and 641 feet in width. In addition to the carving, the visitor complex includes the Indian Museum of North America, an Educational and Cultural Center, and the sculptor's workshop.

South Dakotans continue to struggle with the forces of nature. During the spring of 1997, several rivers flooded. The floodwaters caused millions of dollars of damage to crops, farms and homes. Then, during the summer of 2000, over 80,000 acres of the Black Hills National Forest burned. It was the biggest forest fire in that area in at least 100 years.

Whether their ancestors hunted bison or mined gold, South Dakotans are trying to improve life in their state. They're working to keep children healthy, to update the technology available in the state's schools, and to clean up their state's land and air.

PEOPLE & ECONOMY

Gold Mines, Green Pastures

Most South Dakotans grow up on farms, on ranches, or in small towns. Some of South Dakota's 755,000 residents still work the land their families homesteaded in the late 1800s and early 1900s.

About 1 out of 11 workers in South Dakota has a job in agriculture—a large number compared to most other states. Livestock brings in the most money for South Dakota's farmers and ranchers.

Dairy cattle, chickens, turkeys, and geese are found throughout the Prairie region, while sheep and beef cattle graze the pastures of the Great Plains. Bison, nearly extinct 100 years ago, are being raised on ranches. The ranchers sell their bison meat to restaurants and grocery stores around the nation.

Fields of sunflowers can be found in South Dakota's Prairie region.

Bison meat is lower in fat and cholesterol than beef. Raising bison on ranches is a growing industry in South Dakota.

South Dakota's leading crops are corn, soybeans, and wheat. Rainfall is so undependable in South Dakota that farmers channel water from the ground and from reservoirs to their fields. This process, called **irrigation**, has saved many crops during the state's frequent droughts.

Along with the struggles against weather conditions, some farmers are having a hard time making a living. The number of farms in the Midwest is decreasing each year. Fewer young farmers get into the business because of the high cost of land, machinery, seed, and fertilizers and because of the risky nature of the job. Large farms owned by corporations are becoming more common in the United States.

In 1998 South Dakotans passed an amendment to their state constitution that makes farms owned by corporations illegal. Such laws help family farms in South Dakota stay in business.

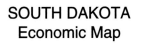

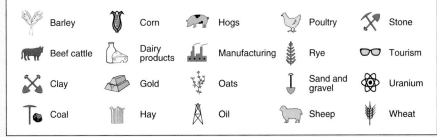

SOUTH DAKOTA
Economic Map

The symbols on this map show where different economic activities take place in South Dakota. The legend below explains what each symbol stands for.

Barley	Corn	Hogs	Poultry	Stone
Beef cattle	Dairy products	Manufacturing	Rye	Tourism
Clay	Gold	Oats	Sand and gravel	Uranium
Coal	Hay	Oil	Sheep	Wheat

Barns like this one are a common sight throughout South Dakota's farm country.

Crops and livestock are taken to the state's food-processing companies, where workers package meat and dairy products and grind grain into flour or livestock feed. Some South Dakotans build farm machinery, computers, and construction equipment. Other kinds of goods made in the state include electrical components for computers, lumber products, and gold jewelry. About 1 in every 10 working South Dakotans has a job in manufacturing.

Mines throughout the state employ only 1 percent of South Dakota's workforce. The Homestake Gold Mine in the Black Hills produces the most gold in the state. Western South Dakota also yields large amounts of oil.

The people who sell South Dakota's minerals have what are called service jobs. People with service jobs also include bankers, doctors, and restaurant employees. Service businesses employ about three out of five of the state's workers.

The Homestake Gold Mine in Lead, South Dakota, continues to produce gold after more than 100 years.

The state capitol building in Pierre is the center of South Dakotan government.

South Dakota's service jobs are found mostly in the state's largest cities, which include Sioux Falls, Rapid City, and Aberdeen. Many government workers, including the governor, live in the state capital of Pierre. Other government workers include soldiers and park rangers. About 14 percent of working South Dakotans are employees of the state or federal government.

Most South Dakotans have ancestors from Norway, Sweden, Denmark, Canada, Great Britain, Germany, and Russia. African Americans and Asian Americans each make up less than 1 percent of the state's population, while Latinos make up just over 1 percent.

Native Americans in South Dakota number more

than 60,000—about 8 percent of the state's total population. Some Native Americans live on the state's nine Indian reservations, which include two of the largest reservations in the United States— Pine Ridge and Cheyenne River.

In the Black Hills, not too far from the Pine Ridge Indian Reservation, sculptors are building a memorial to Crazy Horse, one of the greatest leaders in Sioux history. When it is finished, the Crazy Horse Memorial will stand 563 feet high and 641 feet long. It will be the largest statue in the world.

Children from Pine Ridge Indian Reservation, one of the nation's largest reservations, spend the day at an amusement park.

In 1991 South Dakota celebrated the 50th anniversary of another Black Hills attraction, the Mount Rushmore National Memorial. One year later, South Dakota's nickname was changed from the Sunshine State to the Mount Rushmore State.

Another attraction in the Black Hills region is Flintstones Bedrock City, a park where visitors can catch a glimpse of the Stone Age and eat Bronto Burgers and Dino Dogs.

The Wild West is remembered in Deadwood and Lead, towns where the nation's last great gold rush took place in 1876. Deadwood still has an Old West feel. Casino gambling in Deadwood became legal in 1989, and taxes from gambling are an important source of income for South Dakota.

Visitors to the Cultural Heritage Center in Pierre learn about an early mining operation.

A grain mural of Mount Rushmore National Memorial decorates one section of the Corn Palace in Mitchell. New designs are created each year.

In eastern South Dakota, Mitchell is home to the Corn Palace. Inside and outside, the walls of the palace are decorated with thousands of bushels of native corn and grasses. Every August the Corn Palace Festival celebrates harvesttime with parades and food.

Northeast of Mitchell lies De Smet, the town made famous by author Laura Ingalls Wilder. In a series of popular children's books, Wilder described growing up on the prairie in the late 1800s. Her original South Dakota home still stands, surrounded by cottonwood trees that were planted by the Ingalls family.

Festivals featuring traditional Native American arts and crafts include the Northern Plains Tribal Arts Show in Sioux Falls and traditional powwows throughout the state hosted by Native American tribes. The Oscar Howe Art Center in Mitchell displays the paintings of Oscar Howe, a famous Sioux artist.

The Ingalls Home is open for tours in De Smet.

Towns throughout South Dakota are proud of their historic sites and museums. The Prairie Homestead & Badlands Trading Post near Badlands National Park displays original homestead buildings. At the Black Hills Mining Museum in Lead, visitors can see how mining has changed over the years and can even pan for gold.

In Hot Springs, visitors can view the remains of prehistoric animals. The animals were trapped in a limestone pit and died more than 10,000 years ago.

Beaver Creek Gorge in Wind Cave National Park thrills climbers.

Just outside Rapid City, the South Dakota Air & Space Museum at Ellsworth Air Force Base exhibits several types of aircraft, including old bomber and fighter planes and a Minute Man missile. More delicate aircraft are housed indoors. The South Dakota Art Museum in Brookings features the work of some of the state's most famous artists.

For those who prefer the open air, the Black Hills region offers ski slopes, hiking trails, and lakes and streams for fishing. The Great Lakes of South Dakota along the Missouri River are popular among boaters, fishers, and swimmers.

Along the eastern edge of the Black Hills lie Custer State Park and Wind Cave National Park, where large herds of bison graze freely. In nearby Badlands National Park, hikers can see the remains of ancient animals that once roamed the region. The bones of three-toed horses, prehistoric camels, and saber-toothed tigers are preserved in the area's colorful cliffs.

THE ENVIRONMENT

Saving the Soil

armers in the grasslands of South Dakota and other states have provided the nation with most of its food for more than 100 years. Some of the farming methods used over the years have robbed the region's once rich soil of nutrients and have exposed millions of tons of topsoil to blowing winds. Some experts predict that the grasslands will soon be ruined unless farmers continue to improve their methods and unless researchers develop stronger varieties of crops.

Corn is a main crop grown in the grasslands region of South Dakota.

Wheat produced on the Great Plains is shipped all over the world.

Farmers have known for a long time that different crops absorb different nutrients from the soil. Farmers also know that if they change the type of crop they plant every year—a practice called **crop rotation**—the soil is enriched. But sometimes the U.S. government encourages farmers to grow a certain crop, such as wheat, year after year by paying high prices for it. Many farmers cannot earn enough money to continue farming unless they plant the high-paying crop. This practice discourages crop rotation and, over time, the quality of the soil is reduced.

Before large numbers of farmers came to South Dakota, Native Americans grew a limited number of crops that hardly even affected the grasslands. Thousands of different types of native grasses covered the area. Tallgrasses, reaching at least five feet high, spanned the eastern strip of South Dakota's Prairie region, where rainfall was the most plentiful. A variety of short, medium, and tall plants called mixed-grasses grew over the Great Plains.

Native grasses are excellent for the soil. When native grasses die they decay, adding valuable nutrients to the soil. The great variety of native plants once found on the grasslands enriched the soil with many different kinds of nutrients.

A bison skull lies in the South Dakota prairie grass. Like plant life, decaying animals provide vital nutrients to the soil.

One bison needs up to 100 acres of grasses each year to live. Bison, or buffalo, are the largest animals on the prairie.

These durable, fast-growing native plants also provide food and homes to all kinds of wildlife—including pronghorn, prairie dogs, and bison. The large numbers of animals that once roamed the plains consumed huge amounts of grass, which encouraged more grass to grow by exposing new shoots to sunshine.

The prairie wildlife also gave new sprouts a chance to bud by turning up soil with their hooves and claws. This process loosened the soil, allowing roots to grow and helping nutrients and water to soak into the soil.

Drought destroys crops and leaves soil unprotected from the sun and wind.

Native grasses and wildlife disappeared acre by acre as farmers plowed the prairie. They broke up the sod and planted non-native grasses, such as wheat and corn. Unlike the native grasses, these cultivated crops could not always survive South Dakota's harsh weather. During drought, crops either died or failed to sprout. The rich topsoil—once held down firmly by the solid roots of native grasses—was exposed and sometimes blown away by the wind.

After harvesting their crops, farmers plowed up the stubble, leaving the land bare. With no grasses left to decay and add nutrients, the quality of the soil became poor. To ensure a good harvest the following year, farmers fertilized their crops with costly chemical nutrients. Fertilizers can pollute soil and water and can increase the cost of farming.

Farmers help prevent soil from eroding or blowing away by planting across a hill instead of up and down its slope.

To save their soil, some South Dakotans are choosing methods that are better for the land. Farmers help hold soil in place by leaving crop stubble on the ground and by plowing their fields in patterns that help block the wind. By rotating crops, farmers are deciding to lose money in the short run to preserve their land in the long run.

A researcher studies the grasses covering this former cropland. Harsh weather conditions and poor farming methods have made the land unsuitable for producing crops.

Many people agree that a change in how the prices for crops are determined—not just a change in farming methods—is also necessary. Many farmers want to be able to afford to plant crops that help preserve soil, even though those crops may not bring in the most money.

Some experts believe that replacing native grasses is the best way to save the soil of the grasslands for future generations. Researchers could then study native grasses to develop new varieties of crops that would feed millions of people and at the same time conserve and enrich the soil. By developing new grasses, South Dakotans may be able to save both the grasslands and their farmland.

ALL ABOUT SOUTH DAKOTA

Fun Facts

No one knows for sure whether South Dakota or North Dakota was the 39th state. On the same day in 1889, President Benjamin Harrison signed the admission papers for both states. Then he shuffled them so that nobody else would know which state was admitted first. They are ranked alphabetically, making South Dakota number 40.

The longest tyrannosaur bones ever discovered were found near Faith, South Dakota, in 1990. The dinosaur was 40 feet long and probably weighed about six tons when it was alive.

Benjamin Harrison

Custer State Park in western South Dakota is home to about 1,500 bison, one of the largest publicly owned buffalo herds in the world.

In 1972 heavy rains in Rapid City caused the worst flash flood in South Dakota's history. The flooding killed 237 people and damaged property worth $164 million.

Sculptors used dynamite and drills to shape Mount Rushmore National Memorial near Rapid City, South Dakota. The mountainside carving, which features the faces of Presidents George Washington, Thomas Jefferson, Theodore Roosevelt, and Abraham Lincoln, stands 60 feet tall. The noses alone are each about 20 feet long.

Tumbleweed did not exist in North America until the 1870s. Russian immigrants accidentally brought seeds of the spiny, sharp-leaved plant to South Dakota on their clothing. Settlers gave various names to tumbleweed, including Russian cactus, Russian thistle, and wind witch.

The geographic center of the United States is located 17 miles west of Castle Rock, South Dakota. Geographers have calculated that this spot is located exactly in the middle of all 50 states.

STATE SONG

South Dakota's official state song is a lively marching tune. It was adopted in 1943 after it won a state song contest.

HAIL, SOUTH DAKOTA

Words and music by Deecort Hammitt

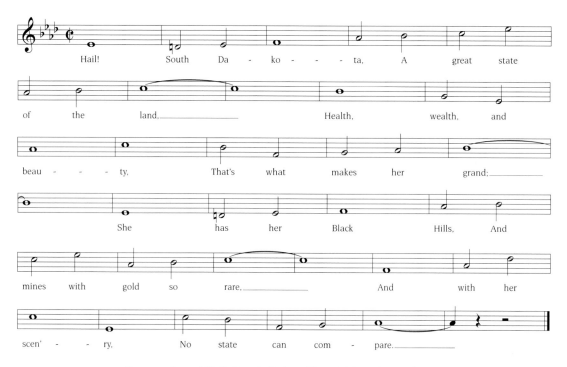

You can hear "Hail, South Dakota" by visiting this website:
<http://www.state.sd.us/state/sdsym.htm>

A SOUTH DAKOTA RECIPE

Wojapi, or berry pudding, is a popular dessert of the Lakota (Sioux) in South Dakota and among other Plains Indians. Recipes for the pudding vary from cook to cook. The original dish used chokecherries, but you can use blueberries, strawberries, raspberries, or any other type of berry.

WOJAPI (BERRY PUDDING)

4 pounds berries (approximately 2 cups)

4 cups water

2 cups sugar

2 tablespoons cornstarch or arrowroot (you can also use ¼ cup flour)

1. Mash fruit.
2. Put mashed fruit, sugar, and 3 cups water into saucepan. Bring mixture slowly to a boil over medium heat.
3. Mix the remaining 1 cup of water, a small bit at a time, with cornstarch or arrowroot until mixture is creamy.
4. Remove fruit mixture from heat.
5. Add cornstarch or arrowroot mixture. Stir until there are no lumps.
6. Place saucepan back on low heat. Cook, stirring occasionally, until pudding is thick.
7. Let cool and serve with ice cream, angel food cake, or traditional frybread.

HISTORICAL TIMELINE

8,000 B.C. People first move into the region of South Dakota.

A.D. 500 Mound builders settle along the Missouri River.

1682 René-Robert Cavelier, Sieur de La Salle, claims the land drained by the Mississippi River, including the South Dakota region, for France.

1743 The La Vérendrye brothers explore South Dakota.

1803 The United States acquires the Dakotas through the Louisiana Purchase.

1861 The U.S. Congress creates the Dakota Territory.

1868 The Great Sioux Reservation is created.

1874 Gold is discovered in the Black Hills.

1876 War for the Black Hills (1876–1877) begins.

1889 South Dakota becomes the 40th state on November 2.

1890 The massacre at Wounded Knee takes place.

1897 A severe drought ends.

1927 Gutzon Borglum beings work on Mount Rushmore.

1930 A long drought made worse by dust storms and grasshopper plagues begins.

1944 Construction of four dams, as part of the Pick-Sloan Missouri Basin Program, is approved.

1973 Indians take over Wounded Knee for 71 days.

1980 The U.S. Supreme Court orders the federal government to pay $120 million to eight Sioux tribes for land seized in 1876.

1992 South Dakota is re-nicknamed the Mount Rushmore State.

1998 Farms run by corporations are outlawed in South Dakota.

2000 Forest fires destroy thousands of acres of the Black Hills National Forest.

2001 Senator Tom Daschle of South Dakota becomes majority leader of the U.S. Senate.

OUTSTANDING SOUTH DAKOTANS

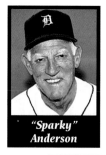

"Sparky"
Anderson

George Lee ("Sparky") Anderson (born 1934), managed the Cincinnati Reds baseball team from 1970 to 1978 and the Detroit Tigers from 1979 until 1995. Anderson, born in Bridgewater, is the first manager in major league baseball to win more than 800 games with two different teams. He is also the first manager ever to win a World Series in both the American and National leagues.

Tom Brokaw

Tom Brokaw (born 1940) is recognized by millions of Americans as the anchor on *NBC Nightly News*. Before taking the position in 1982, Brokaw hosted NBC's early morning news program, the *Today* show. He was raised in Webster, South Dakota.

Vera Cleaver

Vera Cleaver (1919–1992) from Virgil, South Dakota, is an award-winning author of children's books, many of which she wrote with her husband, Bill. Her titles include *Ellen Grae, Where the Lilies Bloom,* and *Moon Lake Angel.*

Crazy Horse (1844?–1877), born on Rapid Creek in the Black Hills of South Dakota, fought to recapture Sioux land taken by the U.S. government. Crazy Horse's Sioux name (Tashuncauitco) is more accurately translated as Unbroken Horse.

Vine Deloria Jr.

Vine Deloria Jr. (born 1933), a Sioux educator, lawyer, and author, is dedicated to the struggle for Native American rights. Among his books are *Custer Died for Your Sins: An Indian Manifesto; Behind the Trail of Broken Treaties;* and *Native American Animal Stories.* He is from Martin, South Dakota.

Judith Evelyn (1913–1967) was an actress best known for her portrayals of high-strung women. Among her stage credits are *Angel Street*, *A Streetcar Named Desire*, and *Pygmalion*. Born in Seneca, South Dakota, Evelyn also appeared in several films, including *The Brothers Karamazov* and *Rear Window*.

Judith Evelyn

Mary Hart (born 1950) is cohost of the weeknight television program *Entertainment Tonight*, which features news about the entertainment industry. Hart, who has cohosted the show since 1982, is from Sioux Falls, South Dakota.

Mary Hart

Oscar Howe (1915–1983), an internationally known Yankton Sioux artist, painted in a unique style that reflected the traditional values and beliefs of the Sioux. Howe, born on the Crow Creek Reservation in South Dakota, taught creative art at the University of South Dakota. For over twenty years, he designed the corn mosaics that decorate the Corn Palace in Mitchell.

Oscar Howe

Hubert Humphrey (1911–1978) served as vice president of the United States in the 1960s under Lyndon B. Johnson. Born in Wallace, South Dakota, Humphrey later moved to Minnesota, the state he represented as a U.S. senator both before and after his term as vice president.

Roy Justus (1901–1984) was an internationally recognized political cartoonist from Avon, South Dakota. During his 50-year career, Justus drew cartoons that delivered messages about topics ranging from nuclear weapons to population growth.

Hubert Humphrey

Cheryl Ladd

Rose Wilder Lane

George McGovern

Russell Means

Cheryl Ladd (born 1951), from Huron, South Dakota, became famous when she costarred as a detective on the popular 1970s television series "Charlie's Angels." Ladd's film credits include *Grace Kelly, Now and Forever,* and *The Haunting of Lisa.* Ladd costarred in the *One West Waikiki,* a television drama that takes place in Hawaii.

Rose Wilder Lane (1887–1968) was a writer born to pioneers in De Smet, South Dakota. Her most famous novel, *Let the Hurricane Roar,* is for children. Lane cowrote *On the Way Home* with her mother, Laura Ingalls Wilder, who is best known as the author of *Little House on the Prairie* and other popular children's books.

George McGovern (born 1922), from Avon, South Dakota, served his state for more than 20 years as a U.S. representative and as a U.S. senator. In 1972 McGovern ran for U.S. president and lost the election to Richard Nixon.

Russell Means (born 1939) was a leader of the American Indian Movement (AIM), an organization dedicated to fighting for the rights of Native Americans, from 1969 to 1988. Born on the Pine Ridge Indian Reservation in South Dakota, Means participated in the 71-day siege of Wounded Knee in 1973. He also starred in the film *The Last of the Mohicans.*

Allen Neuharth (born 1924) founded the national newspaper *USA Today* in 1982. He served as chairman of the Gannett Company, Inc., the largest newspaper publisher in the country. In 1989 he started the Freedom Forum, an organization that helps support freedom of speech. Neuharth was born in Eureka, South Dakota.

Alton Ochsner (1896–1981), was a native of Kimball, South Dakota. In the 1940s, he became one of the first physicians to link smoking with lung cancer. The world-famous heart surgeon also cofounded a clinic that later became part of the Ochsner Medical Institutions in New Orleans, Louisiana.

Alton Ochsner

Charles ("Chic") Sale (1885–1936), born in Huron, South Dakota, was an actor whose specialty was playing odd characters. His most famous film appearances include *Star Witness*, *Treasure Island*, and *It's a Great Life*.

Jess Thomas (1927–1993) was an opera singer from Hot Springs, South Dakota. The tenor made his first appearance with the New York Metropolitan Opera in 1962, after which Thomas sang with major opera companies around the world.

Jess Thomas

Merle Tuve (1901–1982) received many awards for his scientific research, which helped lead to the development of radar and to the understanding of nuclear energy. Tuve was born in Canton, South Dakota.

Norm Van Brocklin (1926–1983) was a profession football player from Eagle Butte, South Dakota. He played quarterback for the Los Angeles Rams and the Philadelphia Eagles before coaching the Minnesota Vikings and the Atlanta Falcons. Van Brocklin was elected into the Football Hall of Fame in 1971.

Norm Van Brocklin

FACTS-AT-A-GLANCE

Nickname: Mount Rushmore State

Song: "Hail, South Dakota"

Motto: Under God the People Rule

Flower: American pasqueflower

Tree: Black Hills spruce

Bird: ring-necked pheasant

Animal: coyote

Insect: honeybee

Fish: walleye

Gemstone: Fairburn agate

Date and ranking of statehood:
   November 2, 1889, the 40th state

Capital: Pierre

Area: 75,896 square miles

Rank in area, nationwide: 16th

Average January temperature: 16° F

Average July temperature: 74° F

South Dakota changed its official nickname from the Sunshine State to the Mount Rushmore State in 1992. The state flag shows the change but keeps the traditional state seal showing South Dakota's early industries of mining and farming.

POPULATION GROWTH

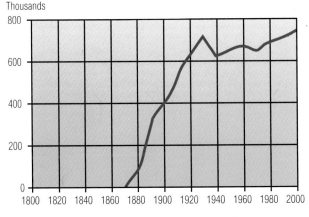

This chart shows how South Dakota's population has grown from 1870 to 2000.

South Dakota's state seal, which appears on the state's flag, shows a farmer plowing a field, cattle grazing, a riverboat on the Missouri River, and a smelting furnace. The images represent important industries in South Dakota.

Population: 754,844 (2000 census)

Rank in population, nationwide: 46th

Major cities and populations: (2000 census) Sioux Falls (123,975), Rapid City (59,607), Aberdeen (24,658), Watertown (20,237)

U.S. senators: 2

U.S. representatives: 1

Electoral votes: 3

Natural resources: clay, fertile soil, gold, natural gas, oil, sand and gravel, silver, stone

Agricultural products: beef cattle, chickens, corn, dairy cattle, eggs, geese, hay, hogs, lambs, oats, rye, sheep, soybeans, sunflower seeds, turkeys, wheat

Manufactured goods: computer equipment, construction, farm machinery, flour, livestock feed, meat and dairy products, medical instruments, wood products

WHERE SOUTH DAKOTANS WORK

Services—61 percent (services includes jobs in trade; community, social, and personal services; finance, insurance, and real estate; transportation, communication, and utilities)

Government—14 percent

Manufacturing—10 percent

Agriculture—9 percent

Construction—5 percent

Mining—1 percent

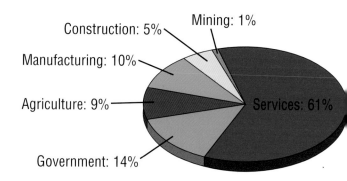

Construction: 5%
Mining: 1%
Manufacturing: 10%
Agriculture: 9%
Services: 61%
Government: 14%

GROSS STATE PRODUCT

Services—57 percent

Manufacturing—15 percent

Agriculture—13 percent

Government—11 percent

Construction—3 percent

Mining—1 percent

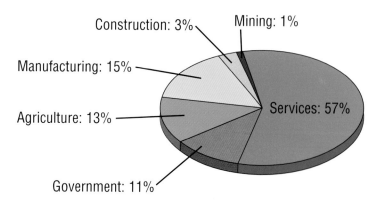

Construction: 3%
Mining: 1%
Manufacturing: 15%
Agriculture: 13%
Services: 57%
Government: 11%

SOUTH DAKOTA WILDLIFE

Mammals: bighorn sheep, bison, cattle, goats, prairie dogs, pronghorns, white-tailed deer

Birds: geese, Hungarian partridge, prairie chicken, ring-necked pheasant, sharp-tailed grouse, wild turkey

Amphibians and reptiles: frogs, lizards, salamanders, snakes, toads, turtles

Fish: bass, bluegill, catfish, crappies, northern pike, perch, sauger, sturgeon, trout, walleyed pike

Trees: ashes, Black Hills spruce, juniper, oaks, pines

Wild plants: American pasqueflower, black-eyed Susan, bluebell, cactus, goldenrod, larkspur, native grasses (including tallgrasses), poppies, sunflower

Prairie chicken *(above)*
Flowering cactus *(below)*

PLACES TO VISIT

Badlands National Park

The Badlands in southwestern South Dakota consist of thousands of acres of breathtaking buttes and mixed-grass prairie. Over 1 million campers and hikers visit the Badlands each year.

Black Hills National Forest

The Black Hills National Forest, in western South Dakota, is a million-acre area of dense trees surrounded by grasses. The landscape also contains canyons and streams. The Black Hills are a prime spot to camp, hike, fish, and go on trail rides.

Corn Palace, Mitchell

The outside of the Corn Palace is decorated with murals made of corn, wheat, grasses, and oats. The murals, which depict important aspects of life in South Dakota, are torn down and replaced each year. Inside, the Corn Palace hosts stage shows, sports events, and other public gatherings.

Crazy Horse Memorial, Black Hills

This sculpture of Chief Crazy Horse will be the world's largest sculpture when it is finished. Begun in 1948, the sculpture is a tribute to the Sioux chief and to all Native Americans.

Deadwood and Lead, Black Hills

Deadwood retains its Old West feel. Its Main Street is packed with casinos. Visitors to Lead can pan for gold at the Black Hills Mining Museum and take a tour of Homestake Gold Mine.

Great Lakes of South Dakota

Lakes Oahe, Sharpe, Francis Case, and Lewis and Clark in central South Dakota are human-made reservoirs along the Missouri River. They attract water-skiers, swimmers, and fishers.

The Ingalls Home, De Smet

The house where writer and pioneer Laura Ingalls Wilder and her family lived in the late 1800s is a museum for *Little House* fans. Tours of De Smet feature historic sites related to Laura and her family.

Jewel Cave National Monument, near Custer

Jewel Cave is the third longest cave in the world. Explorers can tour the cave to see its stalactites, stalagmites—and bats.

Mount Rushmore National Memorial, near Rapid City

Called the "Shrine of Democracy," these faces of U.S. presidents are carved 500 feet up on the side of a mountain. The Avenue of Flags guides visitors to trails to view the massive sculpture.

Wall Drug, Wall

This historic drugstore became famous by giving away free ice water to parched travelers during the Great Depression. Situated in a strip mall with western-themed souvenir shops, Wall Drug features homemade doughnuts, five-cent coffee, ice water (still free), and family entertainment.

Wind Cave National Park, near Hot Springs

Campers and hikers can explore Wind Cave, one of the world's most complex caves. The park contains forests, mixed-grass prairies, and wildlife, including bison and coyote.

ANNUAL EVENTS

Schmeckfest, Freeman—*March*

Crazy Horse Volksmarch, Crazy Horse—*June*

Laura Ingalls Wilder Pageant, De Smet—*June–July*

Summer Arts Festival, Brookings—*July*

Days of '76, Deadwood—*August*

Corn Palace Festival, Mitchell—*August*

State Fair, Huron—*August–September*

Cheyenne River Sioux Tribe Fair, Rodeo, and Powwow, Eagle Butte—*September*

Buffalo Roundup, Custer State Park—*October*

Capital Christmas Trees, Pierre—*November–December*

Fort Sisseton Frontier Christmas, Fort Sisseton—*December*

LEARN MORE ABOUT SOUTH DAKOTA

BOOKS

General

Fradin, Dennis Brindell and Judith Bloom Fradin. *South Dakota.* Danbury, CT: Children's Press, 1997.

Lepthien, Emilie U. *South Dakota.* Chicago: Childrens Press, 1996. For older readers.

Thompson, Kathleen. *South Dakota.* Austin, TX: Raintree/Steck Vaughn, 1996.

Special Interest

Cunningham, Chet. *Chief Crazy Horse.* Minneapolis: Lerner Publications Company, 2000. A biography of Chief Crazy Horse, the Oglala Sioux chief who led Plains Indian warriors to victory at the Battle of Little Bighorn. For older readers.

Owens, Thomas S. *Mount Rushmore.* New York: Rosen Publishing Group, 1997. An easy-to-read book that tells the story of how Mount Rushmore became the world's largest sculpture.

Rice, Jr., Earle. *The Battle of the Little Bighorn.* San Diego: Lucent Books, Inc., 1998. For older readers. Detailed story of Custer's most famous battle against the Plains Indians, including why and where the groups fought in South Dakota.

Wasdworth, Ginger. *Laura Ingalls Wilder: Storyteller of the Prairie.* Minneapolis: Lerner Publications Company, 1997. This biography tells the story of Laura Ingalls Wilder, author of the *Little House* books who lived for part of her life in De Smet, South Dakota. The book also covers Laura's relationship with another famous South Dakotan, her daughter Rose Wilder Lane.

Fiction

Armstrong, Jennifer. *Black-Eyed Susan.* New York: Crown Publishers, Inc., 1995. This novel describes a day in Dakota Territory when ten-year-old Susie arrives to homestead with her parents. Black-and-white illustrations and realistic dialogue add to her story.

Wilder, Laura Ingalls. *By the Shores of Silver Lake.* New York: HarperTrophy, 1973. This is the first of Wilder's *Little House* books that take place in South Dakota. The Ingalls family are among the first settlers to move to the new town of De Smet. Here, Pa farms, Mary goes blind, and Laura meets her future husband, Almanzo Wilder. Illustrated by Garth Williams.

Wilder, Laura Ingalls. *The Long Winter.* New York: HarperTrophy, 1971. The residents of De Smet, including the Ingalls family, are starving during a long, harsh winter. Almanzo Wilder helps save the family by finding wheat. Illustrated by Garth Williams.

WEBSITES

South Dakota's Home Page
<http://www.state.sd.us>
South Dakota's official website has links to travel and parks, government, business, and state news websites.

South Dakota Travel Information
<http://www.travelsd.com/>
This site offers information on state history, parks and monuments, attractions, events, and activities.

Laura Ingalls Wilder Memorial Society, Inc.
<http://www.liwms.com>
This site honors writer Laura Ingalls Wilder and her books about pioneer life in South Dakota, Minnesota, and Kansas.

South Dakota Magazine
<http://www.sodakmag.com>
The on-line version of the state's magazine has articles on lifestyle, culture, history, arts, and nature.

South Dakota Public Broadcasting
<http://www.sdpb.org>
News and information about South Dakota from public radio, public television, and multimedia sources.

South Dakota State Parks
<http://www.state.sd.us/gfp/sdparks/>
This site is geared to park visitors and campers and also includes a complete calendar of the year's events and activities at state parks.

PRONUNCIATION GUIDE

Arikara (uh-RIHK-uh-ruh)

Bon Homme (BAHN uhm)

Cheyenne (shy-AN)

La Vérendrye, François and Louis-Joseph (lah vay-rahn-DREE, frahn-SWAH and loo-EE-shoh-ZEHF)

Lead (leed)

Oahe (oh-WAH-hee)

Pierre (pihr)

Poinsett (PAWN-seht)

Sharpe (shahrp)

Sioux (soo)

Waubay (waw-BAY)

This Wall Drug billboard in a midwestern field is one of thousands. Signs for the popular attraction can be found all over the world, including Paris, Moscow, the London subway, and the South Pole.

GLOSSARY

butte: an isolated hill or mountain with steep sides

crop rotation: alternating the crops grown in a field from one year to the next to replace the minerals taken from the soil by one type of crop

drought: a long period of extreme dryness due to lack of rain or snow

glacier: a large body of ice and snow that moves slowly over land

grassland: a region in which grasses are the natural form of plant life. Cultivated grasses, such as corn and wheat, may be grown in the region. In the United States, grasslands are also called prairies and meadows.

immigrant: a person who moves to a foreign country and settles there

irrigation: a method of watering land by directing water through canals, ditches, pipes, or sprinklers

plains: broad, flat areas of land that have few trees or other outstanding natural features

Plains Indians: Indian groups that lived on the Great Plains (a region covering much of central North America) and that shared similar traditions

prairie: a large area of level or gently rolling grassy land with few trees

precipitation: rain, snow, and other forms of moisture that fall to earth

reservation: public land set aside by the government to be used by Native Americans

reservoir: a place where water is collected and stored for later use

treaty: an agreement between two or more groups, usually having to do with peace or trade

INDEX

2857

PHOTO ACKNOWLEDGMENTS

© Layne Kennedy/CORBIS, pp. front cover (left), 54; © Joseph Sohm; ChromoSohm Inc./CORBIS, p. front cover (right); Digital Cartographics, pp. 1, 8–9, 41; © Ed Wargin/CORBIS, pp. 2–3; © Sheldan Collins/CORBIS, p. 3; © Papilio/CORBIS, pp. 4 (detail), 7 (detail), 17 (detail), 39 (detail), 51 (detail); © Tom Bean, pp. 6, 80; Glacial Lakes and Prairies of Northeastern South Dakota, p. 10; USDA Forest Service, p 11; © Lia E. Munson/Root Resources, p. 12; Kent & Donna Dannen, pp. 13, 16, 48, 49, 50; South Dakota Department of Tourism, pp. 14, 42, 46; Chad Coppess/South Dakota Department of Tourism, pp. 15, 39, 44, 45; Library of Congress, pp. 18, 60; Bryan Peterson, Legislative Media Services, p. 20; South Dakota State Historical Society—State Archives, pp. 21, 25, 28, 29 (both photos), 31, 32; Minnesota Historical Society, p. 23; Smithsonian Institution National Anthropological Archives, Bureau of American Ethnology Collection, pp. 24, 30; © Hulton-Deutsch Collection/CORBIS, p. 26; © Tony Wharton, Frank Lane Picture Agency/CORBIS, p. 27; Center for Western Studies, p. 33; Siouxland Heritage Museums, p. 34; Jerome Rogers, p. 35; © Korczak's Heritage, Inc., p. 37; Lynn M. Stone, p. 40; Homestake Mining Co., p. 43; Jerry Hennen, pp. 47, 51; Buddy Mays/Travel Stock, pp. 52, 56; Mark Kayser/ South Dakota Department of Tourism, pp. 55, 73 (top and bottom); USDA Photo, p. 57; South Dakota Department of Agriculture, p. 58; Jack Lindstrom, p. 61; Tim Seeley, p. 63, 71 (top), 72; Detroit Tigers, p. 66 (top); © Owen Franken/CORBIS, p. 66 (second from top); Harper Collins, p. 66 (second from bottom); Vine Deloria, Jr., p. 66 (bottom); Museum of Modern Art/Film Stills Archive, p. 67 (top); Photofest, p. 67 (second from top); State University, Vermillion, S.D., p. 67 (second from bottom); Marty Nordstrom/Minnesota Historical Society, p. 67 (bottom); Hollywood Book & Poster Co., p. 68 (top); Laura Ingalls Wilder Home & Museum, p. 68 (second from top); George McGovern, p. 68 (second from bottom); Johnny Sundby, p. 68 (bottom); Ochsner Medical Institution, New Orleans, p. 69 (top); Metropolitan Opera Archives, p. 69 (second from top); LA Rams, p. 63 (bottom); Jean Matheny, p. 70 (top).